# Love and Other Four-letter Words

## Winning the Battle for Your Family

Lori Clifton

Love and Other Four-letter Words

Winning the Battle for the Heart of Your Family

Copyright © 2021 Lori Clifton

All rights reserved.

No portion of this book may be reproduced in any form without permission from the publisher, except as permitted by U.S. copyright law. For permissions, contact: order@speaktruthmedia.com.

Scripture quotations marked TPT are from The Passion Translation®. Copyright © 2017, 2018 by Passion & Fire Ministries, Inc. Used by permission. All rights reserved. ThePassionTranslation.com.

Cover design by: Lori Clifton

Published by: SpeakTruth Media Group LLC
www.speaktruthmedia.com

For information about special discounts available for bulk purchases, sales promotions, fundraising, and educational needs, contact by email: SpeakTruth Media Group LLC at order@speaktruthmedia.com.

ISBN: 978-1-7364520-8-0 *(pb)*

Printed in the USA First Addition

# DEDICATION

To my family who I love with all of my

*four-letter words*!

# CONTENTS

| | |
|---|---|
| Foreword | Pg. 1 |
| Preface | Pg. 5 |
| Introduction | Pg. 12 |
| Know Love | Pg. 23 |
| Read | Pg. 36 |
| Pray | Pg. 50 |
| Hear | Pg. 59 |
| Hope | Pg. 67 |
| Done | Pg. 76 |
| Conclusion | Pg. 83 |
| About the Author | Pg. 96 |

# ACKNOWLEDGMENTS

Thank you, Jesus, for continually teaching me how to *know love*. Thank you for meeting me in all of the random and creative ways that leave me filled with awe and wonder. I truly am a "words person" that is rendered speechless in Your presence while simultaneously gushing about Your greatness.

Thank you, Alex, for asking me about the first *"four-letter word"* and for the heart that you have for our family as well as the one that you and Taylor are building – all because you *know love*.

Thank you, Scott, Mali, and Nicholas, for always listening patiently to my *"stories"* before I get to the point – all because you also *know love*.

Thank you Charlana, Chuck and Miss Rose for grafting me into your family – all because you *know love*.

Thank you, Pastor Leon Wallace, for leading from a posture that proclaims that you *know love.*

And finally, thank you to my team of editors who also Know Love, you helped bring this project to life and bring sense to my thoughts! Charlana and Pat, you very clearly *know love!*

Dear Friends – here's to *love* and *more* four-letter words!

# FOREWORD

Our families have been under assault for decades. Today, we see the repercussions of those attacks. Children are rebellious, parents have checked out, grandparents are often overwhelmed, and the moral fiber of our nation is hanging by what appears to be metaphorical rotting threads.

While repairing what is nearly destroyed can sometimes seem daunting and near hopeless, we have an opportunity to turn our families around if we will follow the blueprint God gave us in the Word. The Word (Jesus, according to John 1) is our only hope, and the Word is the One we need desperately to look to in this hour. He is our victory, and He has given us His victory to share with our family.

I love that Lori Clifton has put together in simple terms her thoughts about how to win the battle for the hearts of our families. Humans tend to think simple is not valuable. Nothing could be further from the truth. Simplicity is what will keep us safe in the long run. Like Paul wrote in his second letter to the Corinthian believers, *"... I fear, lest somehow, as the serpent deceived Eve by his craftiness, so your minds may be corrupted from the simplicity that is in Christ"* (11:3). Did you catch that? The consequences of not remaining in Christ's simplicity? If we don't stay simplistic, we run the risk of being deceived like Eve.

The need to keep things simple is imperative in this hour. Simple acts, simple words, simple gestures that come straight from a heart bathed with God's love are what will melt the hardest hearts, change corrupted minds, and turn each one to Jesus. We don't need another program, movement, or organized outreach. We need an army of love-soldiers who can't bear to see anyone spend eternity separated from God.

Lori's book, *"Love and Other Four-Letter Words,"* when digested like the Prophet Jeremiah did with God's Word (15:16), will release a new perspective and change the trajectory of anyone's mind who takes the time to chew her words thoroughly. In fact, the result will bring joy and delight!

God chooses families! They were His first church. They are His legacy, as well as ours. They matter. They are invaluable to Him. Let's return ours to Him completely whole.

In its simplest form, the message you are about to read in this book will bring wholeness to your mind and give you clear instruction about how to love your family to victory. Let's get started!

Charlana Kelly, Author Speaker TV/Radio Host<br>
Founder of Women of Influence Network<br>
CEO of SpeakTruth Media Group LLC

# PREFACE

## MY TESTIMONY

I wasn't a pretty girl growing up, nor much of a student either. I loved fine arts and was overweight with curly red hair and freckles, translating to being a geek in high school terms. I had two sisters that were honor society beauty queens and cheerleaders, i.e., popular and cool. I had a complicated relationship with my parents, and I never really knew why. I would discover the details surrounding our disconnect many years later at the age of 40, but I had always attributed our less than acceptable existence to my defiant teenage behavior. That couldn't have been further from the truth. In all honesty, if you looked at my family during those years, it seemed we had it all together. In hindsight, though, I believe we were really good actors. My family was fractured in various ways, and we were all desperately searching for significance and love without knowing it. There was a battle going on for our hearts, and we didn't realize it, much less, we didn't know how to turn things around into a winning strategy that would unite us beyond our blood relative status.

I lived most of my childhood and teenage years with God as a distant stranger until one life-altering day. I met Jesus in a very unconventional way. It was the winter of 1986, and I remember it like it was yesterday.

I was sitting on a rented sofa in a rented house. Honestly, after three unsuccessful suicide attempts before the age of 19, I felt like my entire life had been a "rental," and somehow, there *had* to be more than what I was currently experiencing. I wanted to "own" my life, be my own boss, and stop feeling as if I was always at the mercy of circumstances out of my control.

It was Christmas Eve, and I had an encounter with God that left me transformed from the inside out. I remember falling to my knees with tears streaming down my cheeks and saying aloud to a seemingly empty room, "I will never walk away from You again." Knowing full well that I'd just met God face-to-face, in the form of Jesus!

That cold December day in 1986 was the beginning of truly living my life in the ever-growing awareness that God, Jesus, and Holy Spirit desire to be up close and personal in my life, and we've talked face-to-face ever since. I've written a book and a companion journal about that encounter entitled *Transformed – the Journey from Despair to Extreme Hope* if you'd like more details about my testimony.

As a result of that life-altering experience, I've discovered that transformed people transform families, who transform towns, cities, and nations. These utterly changed people bring the reality of heaven to earth with restorative love.

My Dad was 53 years old when he met Jesus, the same age I am as I'm writing this book to you. He had a massive brain aneurysm and several subsequent strokes that reduced him to a very simpleminded state. I used to describe it like this; *my dad lost his mind to gain his heart*, and he came to know Jesus in the middle of what could easily be described as a disastrous event. He was transformed instantly by an encounter with Jesus, and he spent the next 14 years touching his family in unmistakably unique ways. His testimony, while challenging, is nothing short of miraculous, extraordinary hope.

My parents have since come to experience their ultimate transformations on the other side of life on earth as they embarked on eternity in heaven. I want to encourage you with the truth that it's never too late for Jesus to bring restoration to every member of your family as you walk out your transformed life of love in front of them.

I walked out my transformed life in front of my family, which brought restoration to every relationship. I won the battle! Through it, I developed a very *conversational relationship* with God. To win the battle for the hearts of our families, we are going to have to have a meaningful and responsive conversation with God. He has the wisdom and the plan we need to see our families transformed by Christ. With everything in me, I believe that God, Jesus, and Holy Spirit need to be even more up close and personal in your life and family. You see, *love* is the key to winning the battle! Now let me show you how!

"Mommy, what does 'f*ck you' mean?

My introduction to four-letter words.

# INTRODUCTION

## FOUR-LETTER WORDS! OH MY!

Something curious probably happened when you read the title of this book. I'm guessing that your very first thoughts were about all those four-letter words that you're not supposed to say. You know, the ones that got you a mouthful of soap when you were a kid. Those words that somehow made you feel included or powerful while simultaneously heaping guilt and shame upon your head if the wrong person heard you say them. Those are not the four-letter words that I'm writing to you about in this book.

I'm referring to a series of far more powerful four-letter words that can cause awareness to crash in and change everything you think about a subject in an instant. The *awareness* that I'm referring to is simply knowing or understanding something happening or existing. Here's an example: Do you happen to know what book the most read book in the world is? It's not the latest *Hunger Games* novel or *How to Win Friends and Influence People.* It's *The Holy Bible.* If you didn't already know that fact, you now have a new "awareness" that you previously did not. Simple, right? Let me give you some more *awareness* around the most read book in the world.

According to the *Guinness Book of World Records,* the Bible is the world's best-selling and most widely distributed book. A survey by the Bible Society concluded that around 2.5 billion copies left the printing press between 1815 and 1975. More recent estimates put the number at more than five billion. Yes, you read that right, FIVE BILLION!! And this number doesn't account for the copies that have been given away for free, which means that the actual number of Bibles in circulation is unknown. So, as I wrote this book, I followed the Bible's blueprint. The first words that crashed in and changed everything were: "In the beginning God…"

At this point, you might ask, why is this important to know in a book about four-letter words? Words are life-shifting powerhouses that shape everything we think and say. Let me explain.

God is the Creator of everything that has matter and form. Genesis Chapter 1 gives a detailed account of everything that He made. When He finished and was fully satisfied, God put his stamp of approval on His creation with these words, *"It is very good."* It's important to know that God Himself is speaking those very words over you right now as He recalls the moment that you were conceived in His heart. Imagine Him sitting and reminiscing with Jesus and Holy Spirit:

> God: Hey, do Y'all remember the day we created people?
>
> Jesus: Oh yeah, that was an *amazing* day! They look like Us!
>
> God: (*Smiling and breathing a satisfied sigh.*) They were very good.
>
> Holy Spirit: *(Responding with eyes wide.)* Right?! You know, one of my very favorite moments was when You blew Me into them, and they breathed!!

Jesus: (*Clapping His hands together joyfully!*) Yes!! *That* was the *best*!

God: (*Leaning back onto His elbow and resting thoughtfully.*) You do know that one of Us is going to have to go down there. And not just walk among them, right? One of Us is going to have to *become* one of them so they can genuinely *be* like Us. One of Us is going to have to show them how to do this family thing."

Jesus: (*Excitedly leans forward with a clever grin tugging at His mouth and a twinkle in His eye.*) Yeah, Dad, I've got that covered. I'll do it. It's all good."

Holy Spirit: (*With a quick wink that mimics a sprinkling of glitter upon a gust of wind.*) And I'll help too!

Now back to creation! Just like that, *"in the beginning God"* spoke, with what I imagine His first four-letter word could have sounded like, *"ta-da!"* and the world came to be!

Words are powerful awareness shifters that bring clarity and focus while expressing the unseeable atmosphere of the heart. Words create and cause us to become. Our words are the power tools used to build and shape our families. And winning the battle for the heart of your family begins and ends with four-letter words that release transformative power. The first of which is *love*!

Today there is a battle raging at every turn for the heart of your family. Social media, mainstream media, and government-run schools regularly assault the concepts of *love* and a biblical family unit. The very definitions of *"family"* and *"love"* have been ravaged and twisted to fit the popular trends of the day. Family no longer means *"a father and a mother who raise their children"* but has been stripped of the biblical representation of *love* and is now, according to the US Census Bureau, *"a group of two or more persons related by birth, marriage, or adoption who live together."*

According to modern terms, *love* now has various definitions with various emotions, feelings, and attitudes that can be as disposable as last season's shoes. Sadly, *love* has been manipulated in nearly every culture, genre, and worldview, leaving people with a hollow expression that resembles little more than a pop culture slogan: *"I love you, man."* The battle for the heart of your family is fierce. If you forget who you are as a son or daughter of God, the Creator, the embodiment of *love*, fear can easily manipulate and control you. Perfect *love* casts out fear.

I want to propose that *love* is a person, and His name is Jesus. An awareness of this fact changes everything. And, it is excellent news for you, my friend! The battle for the heart of your family is not lost. In fact, it has already been won by *love* Himself. Our journey with a few four-letter words will help you remember Him and who you are in Him. Ralph Waldo Emerson once said:

> *"The mind, once stretched by a new idea, never returns to its original dimensions."*

I want to help you stretch your mind with God's powerful four-letter words.

I am a storyteller. I think in a very multidimensional fashion, much like a weaver of fine fabrics creates a unique textile. On the pages ahead, I'm going to take some ordinary "threads" of conversation from daily life and intentionally interweave "not-so-new thoughts" into them that will help you to learn how to see things differently. And as a result of applying them, win the battle for the heart of your family.

We're going to focus on a few four-letter words intended to stretch the framework of your awareness to "re-member" and re-attach you with your Divine purpose. Let me add an explanation to *"re-member."* The prefix *"re"* can mean *again or back*, and the word *"member"* is *a person, animal, or thing that is a part of a whole*. The four-letter words that we're going to explore together have the ability to put our hearts back together again by way of simply *"re-membering"* and *"re-attaching"* our hearts to the heart of God.

Winning the battle for the heart of our families begins and ends here. So let the adventure begin.

Love is a person and His Name is Jesus.

# THE FIRST TWO FOUR-LETTER WORDS:

## KNOW LOVE

2001 is a year that will never be forgotten for many reasons. The first of our three children would start kindergarten, and 19 terrorists who didn't know *love* would assault America. Radical and weaponized men hijacked four commercial airliners hitting targets and causing carnage that garnered the most significant loss of life from a foreign attack ever perpetrated on

American soil. In just a few hours, nearly 3000 men, women, and children lost their lives. The death toll was more significant than the December 7, 1941 attack on Pearl Harbor.

The setting for this story began in August 2001. We were preparing to enter the big world of public school with our first child, and *everybody* we knew had an opinion they felt compelled to share with us. *"You're making a mistake; Christians should have their children in Christian schools,"* said one friend whose husband was a church administrator. *"You're not making a mistake; Christian students in public schools are like missionaries to the world. This is a biblical mandate to go into all the world,"* said another friend who regularly participated in short-term mission trips around the world. *"Christians should homeschool their children,"* expressed one friend who had already been home-educating her children. *"Christians shouldn't homeschool their children because they're not teachers by education. Besides, homeschooling creates unsocialized misfits who end up becoming creepy unsocialized adults,"* from yet another well-intentioned friend with a college degree.

We heard them all and thanked them for sharing their thoughts with us. We had to trust that we are the parents that God chose for our kids and move along. We decided to give the public school system a chance. After all, both my husband and I went to public schools, and we turned out okay.

Like many big cities, Charlotte, North Carolina, has a history of busing students across town, and I wasn't thrilled about having my innocent little boy on a bus for 45 minutes for a 2.5-mile ride. We were strongly encouraged by the school to *"let him ride the bus, it's a rite of passage that everyone goes through,"* and *"you can't be one of those overprotective parents that never let their children grow."* So, against our instincts, we relented, got him on the bus schedule, and he rode the bus twice a day to and from kindergarten. Within weeks, our 5-year-old son confirmed that we should have trusted ourselves as his parents over our *"riding the school bus"* hesitation.

As always, his little sister and brother, and I waited for him to get off the big yellow school bus at the corner one afternoon. Bounding across the grass, with arms wide open for the hug that he was expecting, he casually asked, *"Mommy, what does 'f*ck you' mean?"*

We had made it a practice to teach our kiddos from the beginning not to repeat a word that you don't know – but rather to ask us what it meant, and then they would know. Our little guy was doing what we'd taught him.

Doing my very best not to gasp, frown, or freak out, I asked him,

> "Where did you hear that?"
>
> To which he replied, "On the bus today."
>
> "Oh, yeah? Who said that?" I inquired while handing him a cup of juice and a bag of Teddy Grahams.
>
> He replied the name of some boy and said, "He's a fifth-grader."
>
> "Right, gotcha. Hey, let me ask you, have you ever heard your daddy say those words?"
>
> "Nope." as he bites the head off the smiling little graham cracker.
>
> "Have you ever heard mommy say those words?" again super nonchalantly.
>
> "Never."

My brain quickly accessed some great advice I had been given years before about "answering the hard questions" that kids end up asking. It went something like this "always answer age appropriately in a way that they're familiar with." In this case, it meant making the answer simple. Here goes my reply to his initial question:

"You know how when we read our Bible books, and they talk about love and blessings?" "Yep." Crunch, crunch, crunch.

"Well, those words that you heard on the bus today are not blessings AT ALL. Our Bible books call those curses."

"Oh. That doesn't sound good," he replied.

"No, it doesn't, and it makes me sad. It makes you wonder how that fifth-grade boy learned those words?"

To which my 5-year-old son replied, *"I bet he heard them and didn't know what they meant. I feel sad for him too. We should pray for him."* We prayed for that fifth-grade boy right there in our front yard, and then he proceeded to play with his sister and baby brother until dinner.

That was it, no more riding the big yellow school bus for our little kindergartner. Driving him to and from school was a sacrifice that I was now willing to make.

It was twenty years ago that God started talking to me about *"four-letter words" and more* than the four-letter word I'd just heard tumble from my child's lips.

On September 11, I was preoccupied with two sick little ones, ages one and three, and we were headed to the pediatrician's office after taking big brother to school. After a kiss and squeeze, I dropped off my son for kindergarten. Today was picture day. He was more spiffed up than usual, which meant that he wasn't wearing the ever-present denim ball cap that was constantly perched atop his dark blonde hair-covered head. Watching that little boy with bright blue eyes and a ready smile walk to class with a backpack that was bigger than he was, always tugged at my heart. I didn't know what image of him would be forever captured on film later that day, but my whole world was about to be irrevocably stretched beyond its dimensions. I was oblivious to what was about to unfold.

My son's kindergarten class watched the Twin Towers crumble on live television, and later that afternoon, my five-year-old was posed on a chair in front of a standard picture-day backdrop. Weeks later, I would see an image of his face, tenuous and streaked with fearful uncertainty, captured at that moment. Another memory of the fateful day that would bring me to tears.

Along with his classmates and all of America, my son was introduced to terrorism by 19 people who didn't "Know Love." It's taken me 20 years to discover this piece of information that, having lacked it, was woven into the tapestry of my life in 2001.

God revealed to me that *love* is a person and His Name is Jesus. *Love* conquers all fear. *Love* won, and it is past tense, a done deal. We need to *know* this to perceive it correctly and to grasp it in our minds with clarity and certainty. The simplicity of His words left me speechless. The terrorists did not *know love*.

God tells us to *know love*. These are the first-four letter words that we must master. Do you *know love*? Are you ready to *know love*? I am!

It is the first step to winning the battle for the heart of our families begins with; Does your family *know love*? Are you ready to help them *know love*?

> John 15:13-27 (TPT): *"For the greatest love of all is a love that sacrifices all. And this great love is demonstrated when a person sacrifices his life for his friends."*

Friends, remember the person Jesus – The Embodiment of *love*, is The One who sacrificed his life so that we could be reconciled to God. Love is a person, not a feeling or an action but a person who is alive inside of every Believer! The awareness that love is a person named Jesus changes everything!

If you can read, you CAN teach & lead.

# FOUR-LETTER WORD #3:

## READ

*"Some books should be tasted, some devoured, but only a few should be chewed and digested thoroughly."*

— Sir Francis Bacon

In the simplest terms, let me encourage you with this thought, if you can *read*, you *can* teach and lead your children and family. Let that statement marinate for a minute.

As the idea of homeschooling was suggested to me when considering how to educate our oldest son, I kept mulling over all my reasons why I couldn't *formally* teach my children. When I took my thoughts to God, that's exactly what He spoke to me:

> *"If you can read, you can teach and lead your children and family."*

He continued, *"If you can read, you can teach. How do you think I've been teaching you? I wrote 66 books that contain everything that you need to know about My character and nature. I'll teach you as you read My Words, and I'll write them on your heart."*

Since you're reading this book, we know that you are both qualified and skilled to accomplish the task of teaching and leading your children and family.

The year was 2006, and *Clifton Traditional School* officially opened its doors. After nearly five years with our kids in the public school system, my husband and I took the leap into "home education" with three children, ages 6, 7, and 9.

Here's the quick backstory. We had just bought a new home in our district's number two elementary school, and we were thrilled! That is until a few months later when our 9-year-old began suffering from debilitating migraines that left him vomiting from the pain as soon as he got home. We went to our pediatrician, who recommended further testing for many possibilities, including ADD and ADHD, as suggested by his teacher. After a series of tests by experts, through elimination, they concluded that the extreme migraines were stress-induced. During conversations with our son, we learned that his 3rd-grade teacher was bullying him. The bottom line was that he was scared of her because she routinely expressed her dislike for his t-shirts with expressions of faith on them. Based upon her actions, her repeated comments about his clothes, and telling him to *"go back to the school he came from,"* it appeared that she intended to see that he failed 3rd-grade.

In addition, our 7-year-old daughter who had dyslexia needed an individual education plan (IEP), but according to the school specialist, she wasn't *"dyslexic enough"* to warrant such attention. To say that someone isn't dyslexic enough to be dyslexic is like saying that someone *"isn't pregnant enough"* to be pregnant! It's worth noting that I am *significantly* dyslexic and recognized her struggles as she attempted her first-grade homework.

Last but not least, my youngest cried every day when it was time to go to school, saying, *"Mommy, all we do is stand in line, and I MISS YOU!"* We were watching our children fade before our eyes, our family was being fractured, our relationships were being neutered, and everything about it was heartbreaking! The government-run school system was devouring our family by eroding the character and identity of our children.

I was crying about it to God one day. The conversation went something like this:

> Me: *God! What is happening to my children is terrible. I'm a cosmetologist, not a teacher. What am I going to do?!*
>
> God: *Lori, who taught them how to eat?*
>
> Me: I did.
>
> God: Who taught them how to dress?
>
> Me: I did.
>
> God: Who taught them not to play where the cars drive?

Me: I did.

God: How'd you do all of that?

Me: *(blinking hard and stammering just a little.)* I don't know. I just loved them, so I did it.

God: I just loved them. (Q*uoting my words back to me.*)

Me: This isn't the same thing. It's not that easy. I can't merely love my children and have them learn everything they need to learn!

God: Oh really?

God: Lori, how'd you learn to love your husband?

Me: I just did. I read Your words and learned that love is Jesus. I wanted to love like Him, so I asked You for help.

God: How'd you learn how to be a mother and love your babies?

Me: I just did. I know what it's like to be loved by You, and I wanted to love my babies as You love me. So, I asked You for help.

God: So, do you think I can help you teach them *all of the things*?

Me: Of course, You can, but why does it feel like I'm about to jump off a cliff into an unknown place? I won't be able to *un-jump* once I take this leap.

God: (*replying softly*) I will help you.

Me: How?

God: I've got some four-letter words that you need to re-learn. These words have the potential to change everything and *re-member* you and your family. Are you up for an adventure?

Me: Yes, but I'm scared.

God: What if instead of being scared, you're primarily unafraid and adventurous? What if you're *sure* and *calm* in who I am for you, and you simply haven't fully recognized it yet? Is that a possibility?

Me: Yes, I suppose I'm not really scared after all. I guess what I need to know is that You've got a plan for this that will swallow up fear.

God: Here's the deal. We conquered fear and had a *plan* for your success before We created the entire world. Do you know that 365 times I inspired the phrases *"fear not," "don't be afraid…", "I will not fear," "I trust you, God,"* and many more written *for you* in My Word?

365 times! Isn't it funny that I've planned an encouragement for every day of the year? How's that for a plan that swallows up fear? Lori, you can *read*, so you *can* teach and lead your children.

His voice was so gentle and magnetic, both drawing me beyond supposed ability and propelling me forward into the unknown while simultaneously filling me with confidence. The fear was gone!

As a result, I discovered there are many resources to help me accomplish my task. I knew that I could read elementary-level lesson plans and textbooks, so I finally felt capable of teaching the little people I loved so much. I remember coaching myself with these words *"You can do this, Lori, it's only elementary school! How hard can it be*?!" And with that, we launched ourselves headlong into the arena of home education.

I discovered their learning styles and was able to customize their education without compromising our children. It was as if a whole new world opened before us, and we were filled with hope!

As for me, I kept reading and taught them to read so that we could all learn together!

When the middle school years were before us, I encouraged myself with the fact that my children were flourishing both academically and interpersonally. They were healthy physically, spiritually and our family was *thriving*! I discovered that I could teach middle school subjects not only to my children, but I'd also joined a community of other home educators and was also helping educate their families too.

By the time high school rolled around, I wasn't about to let anyone else take this privilege away from me. I *loved* what we were doing. In 2014 and 2017, we graduated all three of our children from Clifton Traditional School. Each went on to graduate from universities and ministry schools across the country.

How were we so successful, you might ask? I knew that I could phone *"a friend"* at any time by calling God for the help I need, which leads me to the next four-letter word.

Prayer is a two-way street of communication with God Himself.

# FOUR-LETTER WORD #4

# PRAY

*"Pray like this."* — Jesus, The Christ

Matthew 6:9-13 (TPT): *"Our Beloved Father, dwelling in the heavenly realms, may the glory of your name be the center on which our lives turn. Manifest your kingdom realm, and cause your every purpose to be fulfilled on earth, just as it is in heaven. We acknowledge you as our*

> *Provider of all we need each day. Forgive us the wrongs we have done as we ourselves release forgiveness to those who have wronged us. Rescue us every time we face tribulation and set us free from evil. For you are the King who rules with power and glory forever. Amen."*

If I were to put Jesus' words into my language, this is what the Scriptures above sound like coming from me:

> *"Daddy God, You're the One who sits above everything that has ever been. You're awesome and the center of everything. Let everything that is full-on in Your heart come to pass here where I am. I know that You give me everything I need, so I have no lack in my life. Thanks for not holding my mistakes against me, and as an act of my will, I choose not to hold things against those who haven't handled my heart well. Thanks for always giving me a way out, and*

*thank you that the enemy has no foothold on me because You are the powerful and glorious King of everything, and I'm Yours. So there."*

Jesus set religious folks on their heads with His example of how to pray when He said, *"Pray like this."* He made God accessible through reconciliation so we could get up close with Him again. Prayer brings us close. It's a two-way street of communication with God.

I love Corrie Ten Boom's words, *"Is prayer your steering wheel or your spare tire?"* Praying is simply talking with God on the fly. What do I mean by *on the fly*? At any time regularly. Praying is meant to refine us, refocus us, and bring direction daily. It's not meant to be a *"Hail Mary"* reaction used only in cases of emergency. We have a life of prayer, not just pulling it out when we break down!

When we *pray*, we re-focus our spirit, soul, and body on the incredible greatness and faithfulness of God. I believe the enemy is boring. He has nothing new up his sleeve. He is not going to surprise God or us with anything never heard of or seen before. He is absolutely *boring*! Developing an understanding that "*the enemy is boring*" brings us back into focus and aligns us with the mind of Christ.

And further, the enemy isn't creative. He copies and distorts what God has already created. Not only that, he really wants the attention and awe of God! That's why he tries so hard to appear powerful. The enemy *isn't* powerful. He's not creative. He's just boring.

When I pray, I like to imagine that Jesus/God is sitting right there with me, and we're simply having a conversation. I tell Him about what's happening, how I feel, and what I think. I ask for His perspective on what I'm going through. It's very conversational. I distinctly remember a time when I was praying for my children, and I was pretty stressed about a particular something, and I had unknowingly wrapped a bunch of "worries" in a formula that I called "a prayer." I remember what He said more than what I said. It went like this:

> God: Hey Lori, I love your children more than you do.
>
> Me: Yeah, of course. But God, this is a big deal, so I'm going to tell you how I want it.
>
> God: Lori, I love your children more than you do.
>
> Me: Right, I heard you the first time. But I'm serious here, and also, I'm entitled to a say here, right?
>
> God: Try and listen. I'm crazy about my children. They were mine before they were yours. Do you trust Me?

Me: (*blinking hard and attempting to choke back the tears that were stinging my eyes*) Yes, God, I trust you. How do you want me to pray about this then?

God: Just thank Me for my goodness. You know that I'm good, right?

Me: (*nodding silently*)

God: Thank Me in advance for my faithfulness and perfect provision. You know that I've never failed at anything. Ever! Right?

Me: (*again, nodding silently*)

God: Okay. Would you like Me to tell you what I have in store for your children?

Me: Absolutely, I would!

And the way I pray changed from that day forward. I lean into the heart of God, and I ask for His perspective, and then I agree with Him.

There are 367 references to prayer contained in the 66 books of the Bible. It's as if God made daily provisions for us to have a conversation with Him. That makes me smile with my heart.

If we want to win the battle for the hearts of our families, then we must pray!

To hear God for yourself is your birthright.

# FOUR-LETTER WORD #5:

## HEAR

*"When we listen, we hear someone into existence."*

— Laurie Buchanan, PhD

What a great thought, "When we listen, we *hear* someone into existence!!" I don't know who Dr. Buchanan is, but I love the image of creation that pops up in my mind's eye with this statement because words are *powerful*. Everything in all of creation listens, hears, and responds to God in some form or another. Notice, though, we must *hear* to create what is necessary to win the battle for our families.

A quick search for the word *"hear"* in the New International Version of the Bible yields 1,700 verses that specifically reference the past and present tense versions of the word *hear*! The reality is that God is always close and personal, and He's constantly speaking through creation.

Here's an example from Psalm 19:1—4 of The Passion Translation:

> *"God's splendor is a tale that is told, written in the stars. Space itself speaks his story through the marvels of the heavens. His truth is on tour in the starry vault of the sky, showing his skill in creation's craftsmanship. [2]Each day gushes out its message to the next, night by night whispering its knowledge to all—[3]without a*

*sound, without a word, without a voice being heard, yet all the world can hear its echo. Everywhere its message goes out."*

Pretty cool, huh? I'd even go so far as to say that God believes in your ability to hear His voice more than you do. That's a simple awareness that changes things up a bit. Doesn't it? Based on this awareness, let's agree with God and choose to hear Him. Let's bring this passage from Isaiah 30:21(TPT), *"When you turn to the right or turn to the left, you will hear his voice behind you to guide you, saying, 'This is the right path; follow it.'"* to the forefront of your mind and keep it there in your daily life.

The four-letter word *"hear"* is pretty important to God, which means it needs to be really important to us.

According to Jesus' words in John chapter three, if you are born-again, then it is your birthright to *hear* God for yourself. Everyone with breath in their lungs was created to hear God. I've written a seven-part series entitled *"Hearing God for Yourself"* as part of The Awareness Suite™. If you'd like a deeper dive into that conversation, connect with me directly. In the meantime, this is how to hear God for yourself in a nutshell.

1. Jesus, the Person of *love* in physical form, is the connection that allows you to hear God directly. Period. No seminary degree or job title at the local church building is required to *hear* God.
2. God created you to recognize His voice so you can hear Him directly.
3. Because you are a chosen and intimate friend to Jesus, you can hear God.
4. Since you're a friend to Jesus, you are His partner. Partnership has its perks, namely being a representative of heaven on earth and bringing

God's solutions into the world. An awareness of this truth changes everything.

5. God wants to talk with you, not at you.
6. You were created to be in a close conversational relationship with God.
7. Today *is* your day to *hear* God for yourself. So. There.

To *hear* God is as easy as 1-2-3. Say this out loud so your ears can *hear* what you're about to speak over yourself:

1. I choose to turn my spiritual ears on right now.
2. I choose to believe that I was created for two-way conversations with God.
3. Today is *my* day to believe that I am hearing God in new and creative ways, and my awareness of this changes everything! So. There.

Remembering we were created to *hear* God as our birthright silences the world's chaos and noise and focuses our hearts on God's character, nature, and goodness for His kids. The ability to hear

God is where we win the battle for the hearts of our family daily.

Hope

Hope is a strategy straight
from the heart of God.

# FOUR-LETTER WORD #6:

# HOPE

*"Hope is the fulfillment of our desires before it's taken shape. Hope is that absolute expectation of the goodness of God showing up and showing off spectacularly."*
— Lori Clifton

I've heard the phrase *"Hope is not a strategy or a tactic,"* for years and it's been used by some heavy hitters in this world from filmmakers to politicians and philosophers. I would say these people need an upgraded awareness of what *hope* is. *Hope* is not a disappointing fantasy. *Hope* is my forte! I would like to propose this as a better statement: *"Hope, apart from God, is not a tactic." Hope* is a reality that takes hold of what is unseen and unrealized to pull it into reality by faith. To be convinced of this *truth* changes everything we believe. I say it like this:

"Awareness changes everything! ™"

Here's an example of *hope*:

> *Hebrews 11:1 (TPT): "Now faith brings our hopes into reality and becomes the foundation needed to acquire the things we long for. It is all the evidence required to prove what is still unseen."*

I've been chewing on that *truth* for years!!

The author of this passage is a man named Paul. However, he had a different name earlier in his life. He was infamously known as Saul. It wouldn't be a stretch to have labeled him a *"terrorist"* by the Christians of his time. That is until he had a radical encounter one day with a *"brilliant light flashing from heaven"* that quite literally knocked him off his feet and called out his name! Can you even imagine such an event?!

He was instantly aware that it was the Lord with whom he'd collided, and he was forever changed.

Let's read about Saul's transformational story of *hope* from Scripture.

> *Acts 9:1-9 (TPT): During those days, Saul, full of angry threats and rage, wanted to murder the disciples of the Lord Jesus. So, he went to ask the high priest and requested a letter of authorization he could take to the Jewish leaders*

*in Damascus, requesting their cooperation in finding and arresting any who were followers of the way. Saul wanted to capture all the believers he found, both men and women, and drag them as prisoners back to Jerusalem. So, he obtained the authorization and left for Damascus.*

*Just outside the city, a brilliant light flashing from heaven suddenly exploded all around him. Falling to the ground, he heard a booming voice say to him, "Saul, Saul, why are you persecuting me?"*

*The men accompanying Saul were stunned and speechless, for they heard a heavenly voice but could see no one.*

*Saul replied, "Who are you, Lord?"*

*"I am Jesus, the Victorious, the one you are persecuting. Now, get up and go into the city, where you will be told what you are to do."*

*Saul stood to his feet, and even though his eyes were open he could see nothing—he was blind. So the men had to take him by the hand and lead him into Damascus. For three days he didn't eat or drink and couldn't see a thing."*

Saul, the *"terrorist"* of AD Christians, collided with *hope* and came to *know love* through the power of the Holy Spirit. His encounter was so astonishing that eventually, even his name transformed to reflect the new man he had become. The man formerly known as Saul became a re-created man called Paul, credited with writing 13 of the 27 books in The New Testament.

Consider this passage that declares the evidence of *hope* because we are joined with Jesus.

> *Ephesians 2:10 (TPT): We have become his poetry, a re-created people that will fulfill the destiny he has given each of us, for we are joined to Jesus, the Anointed One. Even before we were born, God planned in advance our destiny and the good works we would do to fulfill it!*

Transformation is the evidence of living hand in hand with faith and *hope*! Even more great news from the former terrorist declares the *hope* that we get to look forward to and live in both now and throughout eternity.

Again, *hope* is not a disappointing fantasy.

1. *Hope*, apart from God, is not a tactic.
2. *Hope* is a reality that takes hold of what is unseen and unrealized and pulls it into reality.
3. *Hope* is extreme and brings transformation to all who *know love*.

4. *Hope* is the absolute expectation of the goodness of God showing up and showing off in, through, and for us.

*Hope* is a four-letter word that once deeply and firmly rooted in you, will change the awareness of your identity and the very fabric of your entire family. The existence of *hope* is a strategy straight from the heart of God that never fails to win every battle, which brings us to our final four-letter word, *done*.

Done

Love Himself has already won
the battle for the heart of my family.

# FOUR-LETTER WORD #7:

# DONE

*"Those who cannot change their minds cannot change anything."* — George Bernard Shaw

Experiencing heaven on earth is about the awareness (perception) of the finished work of The Cross. It's about spiritually embracing *"done"* even though it may look undone with natural eyes. At some point, we must learn how to raise the eyes of our faith to the Creator of the promise before we see the fruit of the promise because we *know love*.

*Metanoia* is a Greek word that means *"to raise the level of your cognitive perception through a transformative change of heart."* Winston Churchill is quoted as saying, *"Those who never change their minds never change anything."* In reality, Winston Churchill was quoting one of his dear friends, George Bernard Shaw, who initially stated, *"Those who cannot change their minds cannot change anything."* Regardless of who said it first, Churchill and Shaw practiced *"metanoia"* with their statements, even if they weren't aware of it. They experienced a *"transformative change of heart"* about their current circumstances and invited those around them to *"raise the level of their thinking and perception"* and, therefore, *"change their minds."*

Have you ever asked yourself, *"What would my situation look like from Jesus' perspective?"* Or *"Do you think that Jesus' perception of your situation could transform the way things appear to your heart and mind?"* Those are questions that are rooted in practicing metanoia.

*"Can you walk with Me in the different?"* I remember when God asked me that question. My immediate answer was, *"Yes, of course."* To walk with Him *in the different* meant that while walking in what appears to be my *lower-case true* situation, I needed to learn to embrace the *upper-case Truth* of what He already provided to me through Jesus. I needed to raise the level of my understanding.

He continued, *love* awakens love. Fear chokes *love*. Perfect love, love that holds no record of wrong, ~~and~~ makes fear homeless. Perfect love sees beyond *wrong* and *penalty* and is willing to pay the cost that freedom requires. As I wrote earlier in this book, *Love* is a person, His name is Jesus. Awareness of Jesus as *love* changes everything. Awareness of this truth is your gift as a daughter of the King. Can you believe that even before you understand it?

To His question, *"Can you walk with me in the different?"* I replied, *"Yes, I can do that with your help God."* It felt like I was in the scene from *Indiana Jones* when *"Indy"* had to step from a narrow rock wall into what appeared to be an empty void to save his life! The path, not visible, was there. He did not see it until he threw dust in front of his feet to reveal what had always been. At that moment, Indy's perception shifted, and his awareness changed the outcome of his situation.

Here's a handful of *upper-case Truth* from Psalm 139:16 (TPT) that I'm tossing onto your proverbial path as it relates to winning the battle for the heart of your family:

> *You saw who you created me to be before I became me!*

*Before I'd ever seen the light of day, the number of days you planned for me was already recorded in your book.*

The plan for your life is *done*. Even if you don't understand it or *know* what it looks like, you get to discover and embrace this *Truth* as you walk it out with God *"in the different"* beyond ways that you can perceive or comprehend today. An awareness of this truth changes everything.

## CONCLUSION

Finally, here's another *upper-case Truth* from the Book of John 19:28-30 (TPT) to bookend what we've been discussing here. Remember the conversation that I proposed God, Jesus, and Holy Spirit were having at the beginning of this book? Consider this as the fulfillment of the four-letter word *done*.

> *Jesus knew that his mission was accomplished, and to fulfill the Scripture Jesus said: "I am thirsty." A jar of sour wine was sitting nearby, so they soaked a sponge with it and put it on the stalk of hyssop and raised it to his lips. When he*

*had sipped the sour wine, he said, "It is finished/done, my bride!" Then he bowed his head and surrendered his spirit to God."*

Jesus' words and the comfort they bring me is how and why I can be so confident about living in today's day and age. Jesus Himself dropped a four-letter word when He said, *"It is done!"* and I believe Him.

Since we behave from belief, I propose the question to you: *"What does your behavior declare about what you believe?"* I know that can be a tough one to answer when circumstances and situations fluctuate, appearing disastrous. However, Jesus (the Person of *love*) is always the same – yesterday, today, and forever. (See Hebrews 13:8) You can count on His finished work of victory for you even when you walk with God *in the different*.

Let's recap the four-letter words.

#1 & #2 *Know love* – How the battle for the heart of our families is won

#3 *Read* – If you can read you can teach and lead your family

#4 *Pray* – Daily two-way conversations with God

#5 *Hear* – Everyone was created to hear God for themselves

#6 *Hope* – The absolute expectation of the goodness of God showing up and off for you

#7 *Done* – Love finished the battle & accomplished victory on our behalf

These seven four-letter words, one for each day of the week, when put to practice in our thinking and behavior, can change the way you function in every single arena in your life. In your relationship with Jesus, your family, your workplace, your service to others, there is room to grow into *"the more abundant life"* that He promised in John 10:10 daily.

I often remind myself that I get to participate with God and Jesus through the power of the Holy Spirit. Even when I don't understand it all and embrace the finished work of The Cross, it is a joy to walk out these four-letter words every day in relationship and communion with our Creator.

To *know love* was always the plan. The winning victory started where every great success always begins, at the very beginning, with the *"Best-selling book of all time"* and these words that crashed in and changed everything!

> *"In the very beginning, God was already there."*
> *John 1:1 (TPT)*

God is the Creator of everything. John Chapter 1 (TPT) gives a straightforward account of everything that He made, including placing the *"Living Expression"* of His Word into this world in the form of Jesus.

> *In the beginning, the Living Expression was already there. And the Living Expression was with God, yet fully God. They were together—face-to-face, in the very beginning. And through his creative inspiration, this Living Expression made all things, for nothing has existence apart from him! A fountain of life was in him, for his life is light for all humanity. And this Light never fails to shine through darkness—Light that darkness could not overcome!*

Do you remember the conversation that I proposed might have taken place after creation, between God the Creator who was reminiscing with Jesus – the Living Expression of God's Word – and Holy Spirit?

God: Hey, do Y'all remember the day we created all people and put them in the garden?

Jesus: Oh yeah, *that* was an *amazing* day! Every one of them looks like Us!

God: (*Smiling and breathing a satisfied sigh.*) That was a very good day.

Holy Spirit:(*Responding with eyes wide*) Right?! You know, one of my very favorite moments was when You put Our Spirit into them, and they breathed!!

Jesus: (*Clapping His hands together joyfully*) Yes!! *That* was the *best*, simply breathtaking!

God: (*Leaning back onto His elbow and resting thoughtfully*) You do know that one of Us is going to have to go down there and not just walk among them, right? One of us will have to *become* one of them so they can genuinely *be* like Us. We're going to have to show them how to do this family thing.

Jesus: (*excitedly leaning forward with a clever grin tugging at His mouth and a flashing twinkle in His eye*) Yeah, Dad, I've got that covered. I'll do it. It's all good.

Holy Spirit: (*With a quick wink that mimics a sprinkling of glitter upon a gust of wind*) I'll help too!

And just like that, *the light* that darkness can never overthrow, burst onto the scene, and the battle for winning the heart of your family, to *know love*, was won! Friend, upon reading these words, your awareness has just been shifted! It really is that simple.

Dear friend, I've endeavored to write this book so that you can grasp a simple childlike awareness of the above four-letter words. It is here in the simplicity that you will acquire, lay claim, and take hold of the fullness of your inheritance through an awareness of God, Jesus, and Holy Spirit that changes everything.

You win the battle for the heart of your family by the *"re-membering"* (reattaching) yourself to *love* and the wisdom that knowing the other four-letter words brings to your everyday walk with Jesus. It's not enough to know something or someone. We must put into practice the things we learn through coming to know the upper-case Truth.

Jesus – the Living Expression of the Word of God, came to demonstrate for us how to be a family. He modeled what it looks like to live face-to-face with God and face-to-face with each other. Jesus *read* the Scriptures. Jesus prayed and taught us how to *pray* in the process. Jesus showed us how to *hear* the voice of God. Jesus taught us about living in *hope* – the absolute expectation of God's goodness. And, He did it all because He knew what would be accomplished and *done* on The Cross. He knew what we would have access to through a revelation of the Truth. And, He knew if we did as He did in the earth, we would win every battle we encounter *and* the battle for our family.

Love Himself paid the price to restore every fractured person and family back to His original design. To *know love* was and is always the goal and the key to restoring every person made in the image of God. Jesus, the person of *love*, has won the battle for the heart of your family. You need only walk it out by demonstrating Christ's character and ways to your family.

Knowing the four-letter words in this book isn't enough. We practice them by partnering with Jesus daily. *"Just do it,"* in the infamous words of Nike.

To daily *"re-member"* looks like this; it is to intentionally bring the four-letter words we've been exploring to the forefront of your heart and to behave from the posture of belief that each word requires in our life. The simplicity of this statement can stretch the framework of your thinking and bring a new awareness of *love* that changes the way you speak and live; it will change everything.

Here are a few questions that will help intentionally focus your mind, will, and emotions. Consider these suggestions as an invitation to a conversation with God the Creator, Jesus the Living Expression of *love*, and Holy Spirit.

Winning the battle for the heart of your family begins and ends with *knowing love*, the person named Jesus.

1. Do I *"know love"* as a person named Jesus?
2. What have I believed about *love* that needs to be exchanged with the upper-case Truth of God's love?

3. Let John 3:16 (TPT) *"re-member"* your heart:

*"For here is the way God loved the world – He gave His only, unique Son as a gift. So now everyone who believes in him will never perish but experience everlasting life."*

4. What are the requirements for receiving a *gift*? Is it easy or hard to receive a *gift*?
5. Do I have to work to receive a *gift*?
6. Do I believe that I can *"know love"* (Jesus) because God loved the world and gave the best love gift ever?

*"If you can read, you can lead and teach your family."*

7. What do I believe about my ability to lead and teach my family?
8. What beliefs do I need to upgrade by *"re-membering"* them with *love*?

*"To pray is simply having a two-way conversation with God."*

9. *I was created to hear God for myself.* Take a moment to refocus on the character and nature of God and *re-member* yourself with the Truth that you were created to *hear* God.

10. I choose to partner with *hope*. *"Hope is the absolute expectation of the goodness of God showing up and showing off in, though, and for me."* I believe that an awareness of that changes everything.

Daily I choose to partner with the finished gift that Jesus gave to my family and me on The Cross, when He came to show me that this was how love won the battle for our hearts.

You can do it; I know you can. Win the battle for the heart of your family, do it now!

Here's to *love* and other four-letter words!

# ABOUT THE AUTHOR

It's a funny thing writing about myself. Just being transparent in this day and age can be scary because it seems that everyone has an opinion about one another that they feel compelled to share. Nevertheless, here goes!

I snapped a picture in front of the window in my office, it is raw & unedited, accurate, and authentically me. I see wrinkles like train tracks across my forehead from 53 years of many expressions. I see crepe-paper lines dancing at the corners of my eyes from 53 years of more smiles than tears. I see freckles from exposure to the southern sunlight that has left its fingerprint on my skin. I see a light in my eyes that is more than a reflection through the panes of glass. I see a smile that is content and confident declaring "I am loved." I like the woman I see.

I've been told, "Because you're beautiful, people won't believe that you've ever had a hard life."

Believe me when I tell you that the description above was not always my reality. I have known pain, loss, betrayal, and disappointment. My life has had its share of calamity and disasters that I didn't choose and could not change.

However, 34 years ago I collided with God, The Author of Hope Himself became my Divine Mentor and ever since He's been teaching me about my inheritance, as His daughter, and how to live "disaster proof from the inside out." I confidently declare, "I will not hesitate to live bravely."

Always learning. Always growing. Always advancing.

Awareness changes everything!

It is my heart to proclaim this message of Awareness that changes everything and Extreme Hope with any with everyone that has breath in their lungs! It would be my honor to walk with you through The Awareness Suite.

Dive deeper into AWARENESS with Lori Clifton at **www.loriclifton.com:**

The Awareness Suite

Hearing God for Yourself

Establishing your Culture with

7 foundational conversations about your inheritance

Hearing God for Yourself is your BIRTHRIGHT

The ABC's of Hope

Exercising Your Communication Skills

Co-authoring with God

Disaster proof your life from the inside out with

The ABC's of Hope

WifI Training - "What if Instead..."

Become a WifI Expert

Connection is never a problem after gaining this "What if Instead…" Life Strategy.

Conversations with The Author of Hope

Putting it all together while drafting off a

Culture of Connection & Communication

~ life strategies ~

www.ingramcontent.com/pod-product-compliance
Lightning Source LLC
LaVergne TN
LVHW011730060526
838200LV00051B/3108